Contents

Introduction

If you are wild about learning and wild about animals – this book is for you!

It will take you on a wild adventure, where you will practise key English skills and explore the amazing world of animals along the way.

Each English topic is introduced in a clear and simple way with lots of interesting activities to complete so that you can practise what you have learned.

Alongside every English topic you will uncover fascinating facts about the creatures of the night. Animals which are active at night are called nocturnal animals. They have special adaptations that help them to survive in the dark.

When you have completed each topic, record the animals that you have seen and the skills that you have learned in the explorer's logbook on pages 44–45.

Good luck, explorer!

1

Super suffixes

Suffixes are groups of letters that we can add to the **end** of some words to **change their meaning**.

defer ⟶ deference

Let's explore what happens when we add suffixes beginning with a vowel. You will discover you sometimes need to double the final letter of the word before you add the suffix.

travel ⟶ traveller

WILD FACT

Aardvarks are amazing diggers. With their spoon-shaped claws they can dig a hole 60 cm deep in less than 30 seconds!

WILD FACT

Although they look like a cross between a rabbit and a kangaroo, aardvarks have no close living relatives but are distantly related to elephants.

Task 1	Examine these pairs of words and circle the one that is spelt correctly.

a digittal   digital

b referral   referrel

c prefering   preferring

d labeled   labelled

e shovelled   shoveled

f clarify   clarrify

Task 2

Complete these word sums by deciding whether you need to double the final letter of each word before you add the suffix.

a confer + ence = _____

b level + ed   = _____

c begin + ing   = _____

d differ + ing   = _____

e regret + ing   = _____

Task 3

Match each of these words with a group of letters on one of the ants, to make a new word.

 ten  ify  lous rol led red

a chisel + _red_ = _chiseled_

b refer + ~~red~~ _tar_ = _referted_

c forgot + _ten_ = _forgoten_

d marvel + _lous_ = _marvelous_

e solid + _ify_ = _solidify_

f transfer + _red_ = _transfered_

Exploring Further ...

Each red letter begins two hidden words but only one word in each pair is spelt correctly. Circle the correct word in each pair.

L	A	S	A	H	A	B	I	T	U	A	L	S
A	O	R	B	I	M	R	R	A	R	R	I	R
C	N	D	T	S	E	O	I	R	W	O	O	D
C	P	E	O	T	P	E	D	G	T	W	P	E
I	M	N	T	I	D	D	E	E	E	J	R	N
M	N	A	C	R	D	E	A	T	S	K	E	N
O	H	C	O	I	E	L	D	E	G	U	F	E
C	A	T	N	C	R	O	L	D	H	E	E	T
L	A	R	K	C	I	R	U	W	E	Y	R	R
E	P	O	C	A	C	T	Y	O	E	R	R	O
W	Y	H	I	L	Q	A	T	U	G	M	H	H
G	F	S	H	R	R	P	I	N	G	E	D	S

Now dig to pages 44–45 to record what you have learned in your explorer's logbook.

i or y spelling?

The way a platypus looks isn't the only unusual thing about it. Look at the way its name is spelt! You will sometimes discover the letter **y** in words where it **sounds just like** an **i**. Take special care to spell these words carefully!

FACT FILE

Animal:	Platypus
Habitat:	Lakes, streams and rivers of Australia
Weight:	1.4 kg
Lifespan:	10 to 17 years
Diet:	Insects, larvae, shellfish and worms

Task 1

Circle the correctly spelt word in each pair of bugs.

a   crypt   cript

b   hysterical   histerical

c   flint   flynt

d   cist   cyst

Task 2

Now add **i** or **y** to complete these words.

a g__m   d s__rup   g fl__nch

b rh__thm   e k__lt   h ox__gen

c wr__ggle   f h__phen   i l__nks

Task 3   **Choose a word from the box to fit each sentence.**

symbol   physical   mythology   platypuses   mysterious

a _____ are marsupials.

b They have unusual _____ features.

c When they were first brought to Europe, people found them _____.

d For many years before this, they were important in Australian Aboriginal _____.

e Today it is a well-known _____ of Australia, appearing on stamps and coins.

WILD FACT

A platypus uses its unusual beak like a shovel to scoop tiny creatures from the bottom of lakes and streams. The beak is soft and very sensitive, to help the platypus find food in the dark water.

WILD FACT

Duck-billed platypuses are mammals like cows, rabbits or monkeys, but they lay eggs!

Exploring Further ...

Uncover five more of these special words in the word-search grid. The first letter of each word is given as a clue.

T	L	Y	X	I	S	Y	X	L
Y	N	N	S	Y	I	M	T	Y
L	N	O	N	Y	O	N	Y	X
P	E	G	Y	N	N	L	P	B
L	L	Y	X	L	I	B	I	R
C	P	P	L	Y	R	I	C	Y
A	Y	S	E	P	X	S	A	S
C	S	Y	L	L	A	B	L	E
L	A	C	S	P	T	R	Y	P

g _____

l _____

o _____

t _____

s _____

Now swim to pages 44–45 to record what you have learned in your explorer's logbook.

Exploring ou sounds

You will discover the letters **ou** in lots of words, where they can make **several different sounds**. Exploring these sounds will help you to become a super speller!

s_ou_th   y_ou_r   t_ou_ch
c_ou_p   furi_ou_s

Task 1

Draw lines to match up pairs of words in which **ou** makes the same sound.

a tour   famous

b mouth   double

c couple   crouton

d you   mouse

e various   pour

FACT FILE

Animal:	Firefly
Habitat:	All over the world, from North and South America to Europe, Asia, Africa and Australasia
Weight:	Under 28 g
Lifespan:	About 2 months
Diet:	Some are predatory, while others feed on plant pollen or nectar

Task 2

Identify and underline the word spelt incorrectly in each sentence, then write the correct word.

a Groops of fireflies glow to communicate with each other.   groups

b I am very curios about how they glow.   curious

c I'd like to learn as mouch about them as possible.   much

d If I could tuch one, I know it wouldn't feel hot.   touch

e However, I doubt I could get close enough befour it flew away!   before

Task 3

Sometimes other vowel combinations can make similar sounds to **ou** sounds. This makes spelling more complicated! Choose a word on a bug that rhymes with each of these **ou** words.

a noun _____town_____

b favour _____saver_____

c proud _____allowed_____

d soup _____hoop_____

e flour _____tower_____

f youth _____truth_____

g tour _____floor_____

h shoulder _____older_____

WILD FACT

A firefly's glow is the most energy-efficient light in the world because almost 100 per cent of the energy is given off as light.

Exploring Further ...

It's time to play detective! Use the clues to help you unscramble these anagrams.

a 60 minutes   **RHUO**   _____hour_____

b Yell   **OSTUH**   _____shout_____

c Home   **SEOHU**   _____house_____

d Opposite of old   **NYUGO**   _____young_____

e The taste of something   **LFVUROA**   _____flavour_____

Now fly to pages 44–45 to record what you have learned in your explorer's logbook.

Changing Words

We can add **prefixes** to the beginning of some words to create **antonyms**.

un mis dis im il ir in

These prefixes all do a similar job, but you have to choose the correct one for the word you want to change.

understand ⟶ _mis_understand

appear ⟶ _dis_appear

WILD FACT

Boa constrictors don't have fangs or venom. Instead, they coil themselves around their prey and squeeze it until it suffocates. Then they swallow it whole!

Task 1 Identify and circle the word in each group with the correct suffix.

a	disagree	misagree	unagree
b	unresponsible	irresponsible	inresponsible
c	indecisive	misdecisive	undecisive
d	irreplaceable	inreplaceable	misreplaceable
e	unlegible	illegible	dislegible

Choose one of the prefixes on the rats to alter the meaning of each word.

mis   im   il   ir   in   un

a ____polite

b ____behave

c ____edible

d ____legal

e ____regular

f ____deniable

Task 3

Write these sentences again, adding a suitable prefix to the bold word to change the meaning of the sentence.

a Boas wait in the trees for animals **fortunate** enough to wander into their path.

_____

b Once they are caught, it is **probable** they will escape the boa's powerful coils.

_____

c They are not strong enough to **entangle** themselves.

_____

Exploring Further ...

Use these clues to complete the crossword grid.

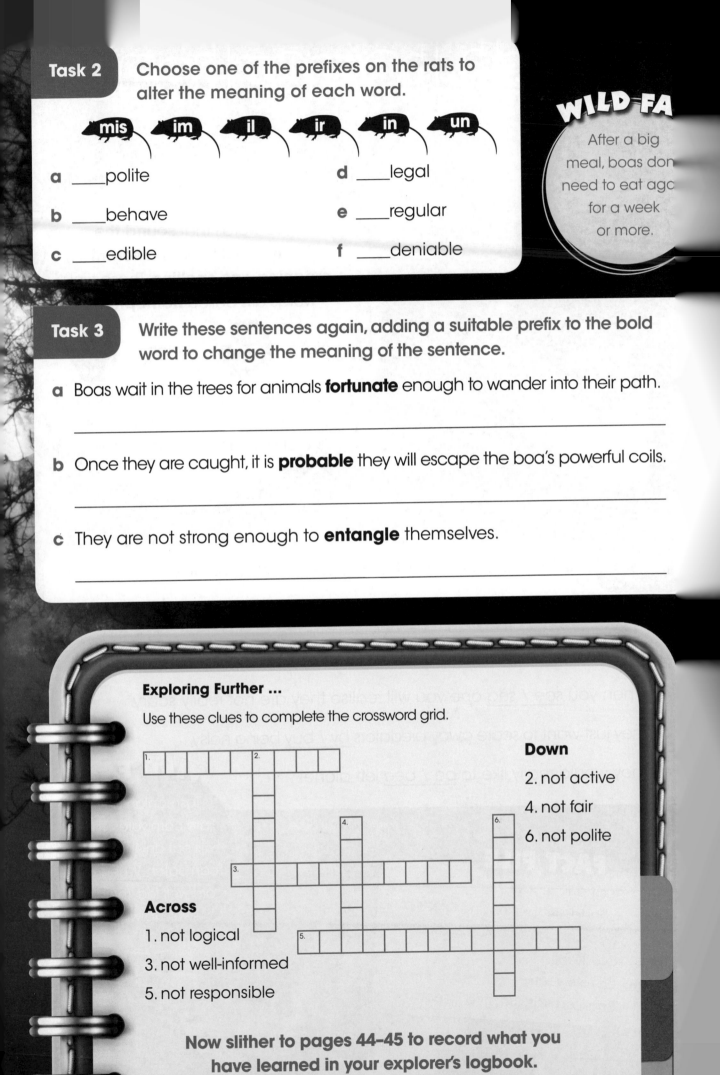

Down

2. not active

4. not fair

6. not polite

Across

1. not logical

3. not well-informed

5. not responsible

Now slither to pages 44–45 to record what you have learned in your explorer's logbook.

Devilish homophones!

You will sometimes discover two words that **sound the same** but have a **different meaning and spelling**. These tricky words are called **homophones**.

night knight

It can be very easy to use the wrong word by mistake, so good writers always double-check their work.

Task 1   Circle the correct word to complete each sentence.

a Tasmanian devils have only <u>been / bean</u> found on one island.

b If you ever <u>here / hear</u> a Tasmanian devil screaming, try not to be afraid.

c When you <u>see / sea</u> one you will realise they are not really scary.

d They just want to scare away predators <u>by / buy</u> being noisy.

e They would really like to <u>be / bee</u> left alone!

WILD FACT

Tasmanian devils are carnivores. They will eat anything they can catch. When they are well fed, their tails swell up with fat!

FACT FILE

Animal: Tasmanian devil
Habitat: Coastal scrublands and forests of Tasmania, an island off Australia
Weight: 4 to 12 kg
Lifespan: Up to 5 years
Diet: Snakes, birds, fish, and insects

Task 2 Circle the incorrect homophones in these sentences then write the correct word.

a Landed in Tasmania this morning. Too tired to right more! _____

b We need to find a sauce of water. _____

c The sailors have eaten all of hour rations. _____

d I would love sum supper. _____

e Your lucky to be at home right now! _____

Task 3 Write two homophones for each of these words.

a saw _____ _____

b pour _____ _____

c vane _____ _____

d rain _____ _____

e rode _____ _____

f chord _____ _____

WILD FACT

Tasmanian devils can scare people wit their creepy night-tim screaming, but they a actually shy, cautious animals which look c bit like baby bears.

Exploring Further ...

Join these homophones to their meanings.

a pare   a type of metal

b pair   a loud cry

c steel   two of something

d steal   a large sea mammal

e wail   to take without permission

f whale   to cut off the outer layer of something

Now run to pages 44–45 to record what you have learned in your explorer's logbook.

Wild word endings

Shhh!
Listen carefully to this. Some **word endings** can be tricky to spell because they **sound the same**.

tion sion ssion cian

You need to learn which ending to use in your writing.

FACT FILE

Animal: Hedgehog
Habitat: Europe, Asia, and Africa
Weight: 397 to 1106 g
Lifespan: 2 to 5 years
Diet: Insects, worms, centipedes, snails, mice, frogs and snakes

Task 1

Circle the correctly spelt word in each pair.

a setion   session

b musition   musician

c ration   rassion

d tension   tencian

e admition   admission

f incition   incision

Task 2

Select a word ending from a caterpillar to complete these words.

tion   sion   ssion   cian

a expan_____   b politi_____   c discu_____

d ac_____   e inten_____   f comple_____

Write your own sentences using these words.

decision _____

_____

invention _____

_____

permission _____

_____

magician _____

_____

hibernation _____

_____

WILD FACT

Hedgehogs wander up to 2 km each night looking for food to eat. Not bad on little legs!

WILD FACT

Hedgehogs have terrible table manners! They are very noisy eaters and can often be heard snorting and snuffling in the hedgerows.

Exploring Further ...

Complete this explorer's notebook by adding the missing word endings.

My pa_____ for wildlife has led me to study hedgehogs. It is my inten_____ to document every aspect of their lives. Hedgehogs gain protec_____ from as many as 6000 sharp spines. Another adapta_____ is the ability to roll into a ball when threatened. This reac_____ protects them from many predators.

Now scurry to pages 44–45 to record what you have learned in your explorer's logbook.

Applying apostrophes

Apostrophes

help us to discover when a thing belongs to someone or something. The position of the apostrophe is important because it tells us whether we are reading about one person or thing, or more than one.

a kiwi's egg

two kiwis' eggs

An important exception is **its** which doesn't have an apostrophe when you write that something belongs to it.

It's always means **it is**.

WILD FACT

Kiwis lay extremely large eggs, which can be up to a quarter of their body weight.

FACT FILE

Animal:	Kiwi
Habitat:	Forests, woods, river lands and bushy plains of New Zealand
Weight:	1.8 to 4 kg
Lifespan:	20 to 50 years
Diet:	Earthworms, insects, larvae, beetles, snails, crayfish and fruits

Task 1 Add an apostrophe to the bold word in each sentence.

a A **kiwis** feathers look more like fur.

b The **explorers** camp fire kept them warm when night fell.

c The **zoologists** map helped her to find her way safely.

d **Kiwis** long beaks help them to find insects to eat.

e The **suns** heat doesn't suit many nocturnal animals.

WILD FACT

Kiwis are only found in New Zealand where they are the country's national bird.

Underline five mistakes in this piece of writing.

The explorers' adventure began when he set sail. The captain's men warned him that the sea was too rough, but he did not listen. The ships sails tore in the strong wind, and it lost it's rigging. A sailors' shouts could be heard over the roar of the storm as he struggled to hold on to the ship's wheel. The storms' power was unbelievable, and it felt as if it would go on forever.

Task 3

Now complete the table by filling in the missing words. The first one has been done for you.

Singular	Plural
a woman's bag	two women's bags
a rabbit's ears	two
a person's health	two
a	two countries' flags
a child's toy	two
a man's key	two
a monkey's tail	two

Exploring Further ...

Look carefully at these sentences. Put a tick in the box where apostrophes have been used correctly. Circle any mistakes you find.

a   It's raining again this morning. ☐

b   Kiwi's come from New Zealand. ☐

c   The explorers' bag was lost when his boat capsized. ☐

d   The bird's beak was long and curved. ☐

e   The mens' water bottles were empty. ☐

Now potter to pages 44–45 to record what you have learned in your explorer's logbook.

Totally adverbs

It's time to explore how adding **ly** to an **adjective** can create **adverbs**. They help us describe how something is done.

graceful  gracefully

Sometimes we need to change the end of the word before we can add **ly**.

gentle ⟶ gent<u>ly</u>

angry ⟶ angri<u>ly</u>

Task 1 Underline the adverb in each sentence.

a The hungry mouse peeped timidly out of its hole.

b It saw a juicy berry shining brightly on a bush.

c An owl swooped silently overhead.

d The mouse decided to stay safely inside!

WILD FACT

Barn owls tend to swallow their prey whole. The bits they can't digest, like bones, teeth and fur, are then coughed up as owl pellets.

Task 2 Now explore these trickier words. Can you turn them into adverbs?

a happy _____

b simple _____

c pretty _____

d merry _____

e hungry _____

f irritable _____

g greedy _____

h busy _____

Add a suitable adverb to each sentence.

a Three baby owls huddled _____ in their nest.

b They waited _____ for their next meal.

c The adult birds hunted _____ to feed their young.

d Their chicks _____ consume whatever they catch.

e The young owls grow _____.

f The owl stared _____ at the mouse.

WILD FACT

Small rodents beware! A barn owl can eat its way through more than 1000 rodents a year!

Exploring Further ...

Write your own sentences including these adverbs.

bravely _____

_____

dangerously _____

_____

curiously _____

_____

mysteriously _____

_____

**Now swoop to pages 44–45 to record what you
have learned in your explorer's logbook.**

Sentences, sorted!

Simple sentences are great, but too many can make your writing boring. You will improve your writing style by using conjunctions to **join simple sentences** together.

I saw a scorpion. I hopped on a chair.

I hopped on a chair <u>when</u> I saw a scorpion.

FACT FILE

Animal:	Scorpion
Habitat:	Deserts, grasslands and tropical jungles across the world (except Antarctica)
Weight:	10 to 100 g
Lifespan:	From 6 months to 25 years!
Diet:	Insects, spiders, mice, other scorpions and lizards

Task 1   Underline the word in each sentence that has been used to join two simple sentences.

a   We entered the jungle after we had eaten breakfast.

b   We were late leaving the camp because I couldn't find my compass.

c   Soon we were hopelessly lost, so we ended up walking in circles.

d   We also got soaking wet when it began to rain.

Task 2 Now circle the most suitable word to complete each sentence.

a Explorers go on expeditions <u>so / after / because</u> they love to find out about animals.

b They sometimes travel thousands of miles <u>unless / if / although</u> a new animal has been discovered.

c One explorer spent ten years searching the jungle <u>until / after / then</u> he found what he was looking for.

d He wrote about his discovery <u>because / so / while</u> he was travelling home.

WILD FACT

When there's not enough food, some scorpions can slow their body processes down so they can survive on a single insect for a year.

Task 3 Write a suitable word to complete these sentences.

a Explorers should check for scorpions _____ they put their boots on in the morning.

b A scorpion will use its sting _____ it feels threatened.

c You may need to be treated in hospital _____ you are stung by a scorpion.

d It is always better to seek medical advice, _____ many scorpions are harmless to humans.

Exploring Further ...

Add your own endings to these sentences, using the bold word to help you decide what happens next.

a We were terrified **because**
_____.

b I crept outside the tent **after**
_____.

c A mysterious shape appeared out of the gloom, **so**
_____.

d I was so relieved **when**
_____.

Now scuttle to pages 44–45 to record what you have learned in your explorer's logbook.

Adding information

Adding **extra** bits of **information** to our **sentences** makes them more informative. It can help us to show **when**, **where** or **how** something happened.

I saw a koala.   *I saw a koala last night.*

We often add this information to the end of our sentences, but it can go at the beginning too. This is called a **fronted adverbial**. When we do this, we must use a comma to show where the two parts are joined.

Last night, I saw a koala.

Varying where we add extra information makes our writing more interesting to read.

Task 1 Identify and underline the extra information that has been added to these sentences.

a The koala bear was sleeping high in a tree.

b At nightfall, the moon rose in the sky.

c The explorer walked through the forest until she was exhausted.

d As she watched, the creature disappeared.

e High in the sky, the stars shone brightly.

Task 2 Add a comma to these sentences.

a After the storm we set off back to camp.

b In the trees the birds shook the rain from their feathers.

c An hour later the sun came out.

d All around us steam rose from the glossy leaves of plants.

e Above us the birds began to sing.

Task 3 Write these sentences again, moving the extra information to the beginning of the sentence. Don't forget the comma!

a Bush fires are quite common in Australia.

_____

b Slow animals like koalas can be injured in bush fires.

_____

c Many koalas were taken to wildlife hospitals after the fire.

_____

Exploring Further ...

Match up each sentence opening with an ending that makes sense.

a Despite their name,   koala bears are fussy eaters.

b As land is cleared for farming,   koala bears are not really bears.

c Preferring certain types of eucalyptus leaves,   koalas' habitats are being lost.

Now climb to pages 44–45 to record what you have learned in your explorer's logbook.

Time to talk!

FACT FILE

Animal: Paradoxical frog
Habitat: Ponds, lakes and lagoons in South America and Trinidad
Lifespan: 7 to10 years
Diet: Insects

Did you know there are two ways we can write about what someone says?

We can use **reported speech** to tell or report what they say:

Louis <u>said he was going out</u>.

Or we can use **direct speech** which is the actual words the person says. When we do this, we need to use the correct punctuation, including inverted commas.

<u>'I'm going out,'</u> said Louis.

Note that the comma goes *before* the last inverted comma.

Task 1 — Add inverted commas to these sentences.

a The zoologist exclaimed, This water is so muddy, I can't see a thing!

b Her guide replied, The frogs will be hiding in the mud.

c Have you ever seen one? asked the zoologist.

d I'm afraid not, admitted her guide.

Task 2 Decide whether you think each of these sentences includes direct or reported speech. Write **direct (D)** or **reported (R)** in the box at the end of each one.

a The zoologist wondered, 'Which path should we take?' ☐

b 'Take the left hand path,' her guide replied. ☐

c The zoologist agreed this was the best route, and they set off. ☐

d After a while, the guide suddenly exclaimed, 'I can see it through the trees!' ☐

e He said he hoped they would find paradoxical frogs there. ☐

Task 3 When you write direct speech, using the word 'said' all the time becomes very boring. Think of a better word to fill the gaps in these sentences.

a The zoologist _____, 'Look at the size of that tadpole!'

b She _____, 'Does anyone understand why the paradoxical frog does this?'

c Her guide _____, 'I don't think so. What do you think?'

d 'I haven't got a clue myself,' she _____.

Exploring Further ...

Think of your own direct speech to complete these sentences. Don't forget the inverted commas!

a As she crossed the high rope bridge, the explorer exclaimed,

_____.

b Safely on the other side, she shouted back to her companions,

_____.

c At the top of the mountain she paused to catch her breath,

gasping, _____.

d _____! she said, taking

in the amazing view.

Now hop to pages 44–45 to record what you have learned in your explorer's logbook.

Untangling tenses

We can use different verb forms to describe when something is done. These are called **tenses**.

We might want to write about something that happened in the past and is finished. This is called the **simple past**.

The explorer travelled for months.

Or, we might want to write that something started in the past but still carries on now. For this, we use a form of verb called the **present perfect**.

The explorer has travelled for months.

Being able to use a variety of tenses helps us to write exactly when things have happened.

FACT FILE

Animal:	Badger
Habitat:	Woodlands of most of Europe and parts of Asia, North America and Africa
Weight:	9.1 to 14 kg
Lifespan:	Up to 15 years
Diet:	Worms, insects, grubs, and the eggs and young of ground-nesting birds

Task 1   Underline the present perfect tense in these sentences.

a People have loved the secretive badger for many years.

b The badgers have enlarged and improved their sett.

c Badgers have enchanted people with their stripy faces.

d A badger has visited my garden regularly at night.

WILD FACT

Badgers are particularly fond of earthworms, and can eat several hundred every night.

Task 2 Tick the sentences which include the present perfect tense.

a We watched badgers playing outside their sett. ☐

b A family of badgers has lived in this sett for decades. ☐

c The sett has grown bigger and more complex over the years. ☐

d The sett was damaged when a tree was uprooted last year. ☐

e The badgers have repaired it since then. ☐

Task 3 Write these sentences again, replacing the bold verb with the present perfect tense.

a The naturalist **studied** badgers all summer.

_____

b She **spent** hours in woodland, waiting for nightfall.

_____

c She **saw** young badgers playing in the moonlight.

_____

d She **wrote** a book about her research.

_____

WILD FACT

Badgers have toilets! They build special chambers close to their setts to use as toilets, so the rest of the sett stays clean.

Exploring Further ...

Fill in the gaps in this chart.

	present perfect tense	simple past
a	has discovered	
b	has known	
c		went
d	has been	
e		flew

Now dig to pages 44–45 to record what you have learned in your explorer's logbook.

Perfect pronouns

Pronouns can take the place of nouns to save us having to repeat the same noun over and over again.

I saw the <u>tarantula</u> and followed <u>it</u>.

noun   pronoun

There are different pronouns for males, females, things and groups. You need to use the correct one.

WILD FACT

Goliath spiders are among the largest tarantulas and can have a leg span of 28 cm. That's the size of a dinner plate!

Task 1   Underline the pronoun in each sentence.

a Tarantulas frighten people because they are so large.

b In the wild, a tarantula can live until it is 30 years old.

c The zoologist took a photograph so she would remember the spider.

d People keep tarantulas as pets, but I wouldn't want one!

e 'Help me!' shouted the traveller, as the tarantula appeared.

Task 2   Circle the most suitable pronoun to complete these sentences.

a As night fell, the explorers had to admit <u>we / they / it</u> were lost.

b 'Someone will rescue <u>us / we / you</u>,' said the leader.

c The group lit a fire, but <u>they / I / it</u> kept going out.

d 'Perhaps <u>us / it / we</u> need more firewood,' an explorer suggested.

e 'Why don't <u>he / us / you</u> get some then?' snapped another.

Task 3 Write these sentences again, using pronouns to remove the clumsy, repeated noun. See if you can replace two different nouns in sentence c!

a The man decided to explore because the man loved wildlife.

_____

_____

b The children lifted stones gently to see if the children could find mini-beasts.

_____

_____

c Humans are often afraid of spiders, but perhaps spiders are afraid of humans too!

_____

_____

WILD FACT
A tarantula paralyses its prey with venom before killing it, liquefying it with a special chemical and sucking it up through its straw-like mouth parts.

Exploring Further ...

Pronouns are very useful, but if you're not careful, they can make your writing really confusing. Read this sentence.

The children bought presents for their teachers, but they left them in the classroom.

Who or what was left in the classroom and by whom? You probably have your own ideas about what is going on in this sentence. See if you can clear up the mystery by rewriting the sentence so it makes more sense.

_____

_____

_____

Now spin to pages 44–45 to record what you have learned in your explorer's logbook.

Exploring *ch* words

The letters **c** and **h** are often seen together in words but they don't always **sound** the same.

<u>ch</u>alk   <u>ch</u>orus   <u>ch</u>ute

Exploring the different sounds that **ch** can make will help you to become a spelling expert.

FACT FILE

Animal: Sugar glider
Habitat: Forests in Australia, Tasmania, Papua New Guinea and Indonesia
Weight: 115 to 140 g
Lifespan: Up to 9 years
Diet: Insects and manna: a crusty sugar

Task 1   Sort these words into three groups, depending on how **ch** sounds in each word. Write them in the bugs.

chief   chandelier   choir   chemist   chef   channel

Task 2   Circle the correctly spelt word in each pair.

a broshure   brochure

b sckeme   scheme

c cashier   cachier

d chambles   shambles

e parashoot   parachute

f chaotic   chaotich

Task 3   Write the correct spelling for each word.

a monarck   _____

b moustashe   _____

c crichet   _____

d caracter   _____

e chamouflage   _____

f cauffeur   _____

Exploring Further ...

There are more **ch** words hidden in the word-search grid. Can you discover them?

M	A	C	H	I	N	E	A	C
A	C	H	E	H	U	T	E	H
C	M	A	S	H	E	T	R	A
H	E	S	T	O	M	A	C	H
U	L	E	C	K	O	C	H	G
T	C	H	S	E	C	H	O	E
E	S	T	E	L	K	O	P	H
S	T	O	M	A	C	K	C	K

machine

chute

stomach

chase

chop

ache

Now glide to pages 44–45 to record what you have learned in your explorer's logbook.

Tricky letter strings

As you explore the English language, you will discover that the same sound can often be spelt in different ways: **ey**, **eigh** and **ei** can all make the **same sound**. Look closely at these words.

*ob**ey** sl**eigh** v**ei**n*

You need to learn when to use each spelling.

FACT FILE

Animal: Bumblebee bats
Habitat: Limestone caves in western Thailand and southeast Burma
Weight: 2 g (less than a penny!)
Lifespan: 5 to 10 years
Diet: Gnats and flies

Task 1 Underline the word in each sentence which contains one of the spelling patterns we are investigating.

a Bumblebee bats weigh about the same as a penny.

b These animals prey on insects.

c The bats catch insects as they fly.

d These bats roost far from their neighbours.

Task 2 Now circle the correctly spelt word in each pair.

a beighe   beige

b feyn   feign

c abseil   abseyl

d osprey   ospreigh

e conveigh convey

Task 3 Write your own sentences using these words.

a reign_____

_____

b surveillance_____

_____

c freight_____

_____

d eight_____

_____

e vein_____

_____

f reindeer_____

_____

WILD FACT

The bumblebee bat, also known as Kitti's hog-nosed bat, is the world's smallest bat. It is around 3 cm long.

Exploring Further ...

Now use the clues to help you to unscramble these anagrams.

a A mixture of black and white   **GYRE**   _____

b The sound a horse makes   **GNHIE**   _____

c 10 x 8 =   **TGEHIY**   _____

d Material worn over the face   **LIVE**   _____

e Questionnaire   **SVRUEY**   _____

Now flit to pages 44–45 to record what you have learned in your explorer's logbook.

Choosing verbs

Verbs describe what different individuals or groups are **doing**.

I *was* there on time.

They *were* late.

It is important to use the correct part of the verb in your writing, even if this is not how you normally speak.

WILD FACT

Spectacled bears are mainly vegetarian and will wait in the trees for days for their favourite fruits to ripen.

FACT FILE

Animal: Spectacled bear

Habitat: The dense Andean jungles of South America

Weight: 100 to 154 kg

Lifespan: Up to 25 years

Diet: Berries, cacti, and honey

Task 1 Which of these sentences have the correct verb part? Put a tick or a cross in the box next to each one.

a The explorer wanted to see a spectacled bear, so he were out all night. ☐

b I did not stay with him because I done it last night. ☐

c In the morning, he noticed that there were platforms in the trees. ☐

d They was all that was to be seen of the bears. ☐

e He was disappointed but decided to try again the next night. ☐

f He slept all the next day! ☐

Task 2   Circle the most suitable word to complete each sentence correctly.

a You / I / They was researching bears yesterday.

b Spectacled bears is / was / are solitary animals which live in South America.

c They have / has / had strong, flat teeth for eating plants.

d Spectacled bears eats / ate / eat mostly fruit and plants.

WILD FACT

Spectacled bears are great builders, using broken branches to construct huge platforms high in the trees.

WILD FACT

Spectacled bears get their name from the markings on their faces, which look like eyeglasses.

Task 3   Circle the mistake in these sentences. Write the correct verb part.

a Nocturnal animals is very interesting to wildlife explorers. _____

b Because they sleeps all day, they can be hard to see. _____

c You needs to stay out at night to spot them. _____

d They is often adapted to being active in the dark. _____

e They often has excellent eyesight or hearing to help them find their food. _____

Exploring Further ...

Add the missing verbs.

a she was ———————→ they _____

b I live ———————→ he _____

c she will ———————→ we _____

d he loves ———————→ I _____

e I am ———————→ you _____

f they cry ———————→ he _____

Now munch to pages 44–45 to record what you have learned in your explorer's logbook.

33

Making nouns

The suffix **ation** can turn verbs into nouns.

explore ⟶ explo_ration_

You will discover that you sometimes need to change the spelling of the verb before you can add the suffix.

Task 1 — Complete these word sums.

a tempt + ation = _____

b relax + ation = _____

c adore + ation = _____

d vary + ation = _____

e admire + ation = _____

Task 2 — Circle the correctly spelt word in each set.

a imagineation   imagination   imaginnation

b realiseation   realisation   realissation

c revealation   revelation   reveallation

d sensation   senseation   senssation

e inspireation   inspiration   inspirration

Task 3

These nouns have all been made by adding **ation** to a verb. Can you identify which verb each has been made from?

a desperation _____

b application _____

c occupation _____

d obligation _____

e registration _____

WILD FACT

Slow loris are taken from the wild to be sold as pets or used in medicine and as a result have become very rare.

WILD FACT

Slow loris look cute but they have a toxic bite, which can be extremely painful.

Exploring Further ...

Complete the crossword grid when you have made nouns from the verbs.

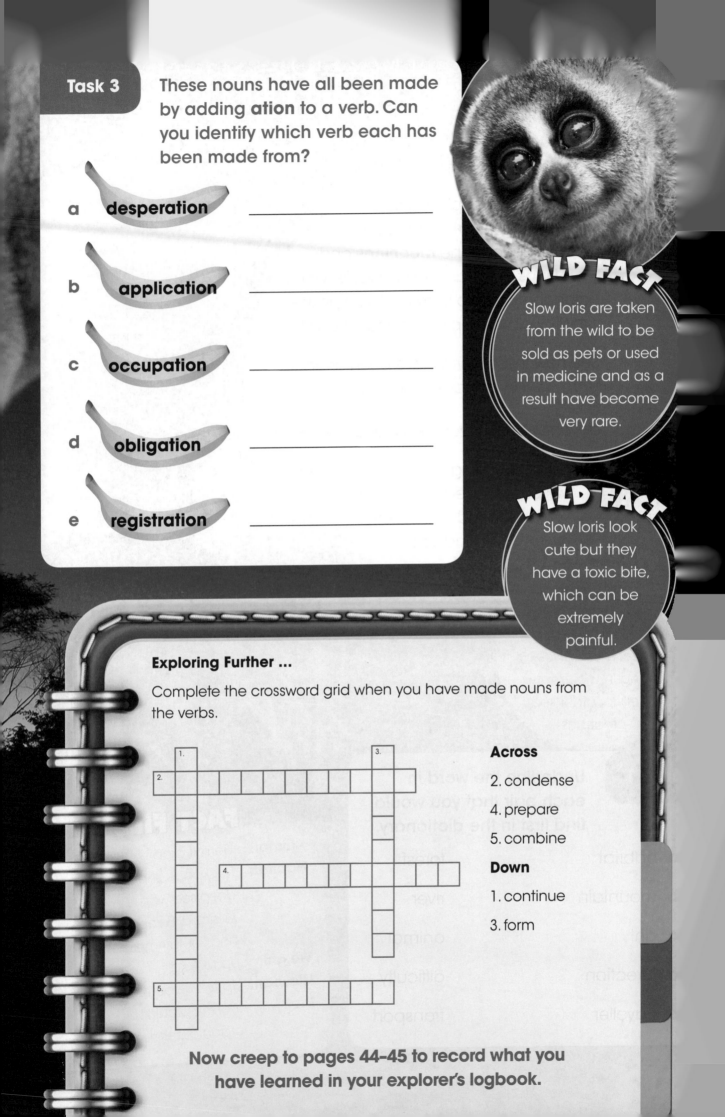

Across

2. condense

4. prepare

5. combine

Down

1. continue

3. form

Now creep to pages 44–45 to record what you have learned in your explorer's logbook.

Daring dictionaries

Exploring a **dictionary** will help you to discover the **meanings** and **spellings** of words. Dictionaries list words alphabetically, so knowing the alphabet really well will help you to search quickly.

See how these words have been arranged in alphabetical order.

adventure   discovery   expedition   explorer

Words beginning with the same letters will be arranged according to their second or third letter, and so on.

Task 1

Underline the word in each pair that you would find first in the dictionary.

a habitat   forest

b mountain   river

c ant   animal

d direction   difficulty

e traveller   transport

FACT FILE

Animal: Hermit crab
Habitat: Rockpools, shores and deep sea waters in Africa, Australia, Europe and North and South America
Weight: Up to 4 kg
Lifespan: Up to 23 years
Diet: Worms, plankton and organic debris

Task 2   Write each group of words again in alphabetical order.

a   nest   burrow   sett

_____   _____   _____

b   kiwi   firefly   hedgehog

_____   _____   _____

c   Tasmanian devil   tarantula   scorpion

_____   _____   _____

d   mountain   mole   moon

_____   _____   _____

Task 3   Think of a word that you could find in a dictionary between each pair of words.

a compass   _____   elephant

b reptile   _____   snake

c forest   _____   frog

d night   _____   nocturnal

e crab   _____   creep

WILD FACT

When a hermit crab grows out of its shell, it simply moves into a larger one. It may pass its old home on to a smaller crab.

Exploring Further ...

Write these words again in alphabetical order.

create   creature   crack   creak   crease   crab

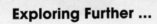

_____

_____

_____

Now scuttle to pages 44–45 to record what you have learned in your explorer's logbook.

Wild World Families

If you look closely, you will sometimes find words that come from the same **root**. These are called **word families**. Exploring word families will improve your spelling and grow your vocabulary.

explore
↓
explorer
↓
exploration

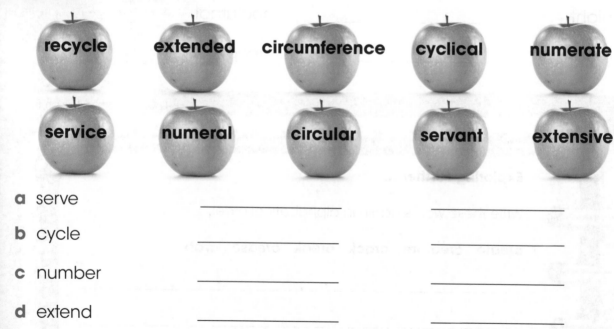

Task 1

Find two words on the apples that belong with each of these root words.

recycle   extended   circumference   cyclical   numerate

service   numeral   circular   servant   extensive

a serve   _____   _____

b cycle   _____   _____

c number   _____   _____

d extend   _____   _____

e circle   _____   _____

Task 2 Circle the word in each group that does not belong in the family.

a treasure	treaty	treasury	treasured
b child	childhood	chilled	childish
c fly	flight	flue	flyer
d aware	awareness	award	unaware
e accuse	accusation	access	accuser

Task 3 Now write down a word that belongs to the same family as each of these.

a dance _____

b health _____

c receive _____

d grow _____

e anger _____

WILD FACT

Skunks warn before they spray! If a skunk turns its back on you, hisses and stamps its feet, you are in for a nasty shock!

Exploring Further ...

Find and circle a word in the grid that belongs to the same family as each of the words in bold.

S	H	A	O	T	O	A	M	R	K
T	H	E	E	S	F	A	R	E	T
M	I	L	B	E	A	L	A	S	H
O	D	S	U	L	M	N	L	E	I
A	D	D	I	T	I	O	N	A	M
N	E	P	L	V	L	I	O	R	I
A	N	L	T	L	I	C	A	C	E
T	S	K	E	O	A	B	L	H	T
L	E	O	D	P	R	E	A	T	H

add

search

build

family

hide

Perfect proofreading

No matter how careful you are with your writing, it is easy to make **mistakes**. **Proofreading** your writing when you have finished will help you to **spot errors** and to find ways to **improve** your work.

Watt a grate idear!

WILD FACT

Squid use their tentacles and barbed suckers to catch their prey before tearing it to pieces with their powerful beaks. Nasty!

FACT FILE

Animal: Humboldt squid
Habitat: Depths of 660 to 2300 feet in the eastern Pacific Ocean
Weight: Up to 45 kg
Lifespan: 1 year
Diet: Krill, other squid and large fish

Task 1 Locate and underline a spelling mistake in each sentence. Write the correctly spelt word.

a I found some informacian about where to locate Humboldt squid. _____

b We sailed sowth across the ocean. _____

c As we traveled, I made notes of the creatures we saw. _____

d The cries of seagulls eccoed through the air. _____

e At night we saw squid greedyly gobbling up tiny fish. _____

Task 2   Write these sentences again, correcting the punctuation.

a Last night we searched for a, shoal of squid.

_____

b 'This is wonderful! exclaimed the explorer.'

_____

c The zoologist suggested Let's explore the ocean.

_____

d Three explorer's hats blew away in the storm.

_____

Task 3   Circle the wrong homophone and write the correct word on the line.

a We guest there must have been hundreds of squid in the water. _____

b I had never scene anything like it. _____

c 'Your too close to the edge!' warned the captain. _____

d I moved back so I wouldn't fall inn. _____

e Its amazing watching sea creatures. _____

Exploring Further ...

Oh dear! Somebody has been very careless with this piece of text. Underline the mistakes and write how many you have found in the box at the end.

It was regretable too here of your intension to abandon you're search four the Humboldt squid. I hope your decision will not be finle and that you will change your mined. Its not to late!

There are ☐ mistakes.

Now swim to pages 44–45 to record what you have learned in your explorer's logbook.

Quick test

Now try these questions. Give yourself 1 mark for every correct answer – but only if you answer each part of the question correctly.

1 Circle the correctly spelt word:

metalic   metallic

2 Chose i or y to complete this word:

cr__stal

3 Circle the incorrect word in this group:

dangerous   voucher   roudy   tour

4 Which word is correct?

inpractical   inlogical

incapable   inreal

5 Choose the correct word to complete the sentence:

The cent / scent / sent of the blossom was amazing.

6 Draw lines to match up the two halves of these words:

sta   ssion

electri   tion

mi   cian

7 Underline an error in this sentence:

The mens' torches cast shadows on the cave's walls.

8 Complete the word sum:

pretty + ly = _____

9 Underline the best word to complete the sentence:

We pitched our tents because / so / and night was approaching.

10 Add the missing comma to this sentence:

In the morning we set off again on our journey.

11 Add the inverted commas to this sentence:

I'll record my discovery in my notebook, said the explorer.

12 Write this sentence again, replacing the bold verb with the present perfect form:

The zoologist **trekked** right across the mountain.

_____

13 Add a suitable pronoun to complete the sentence:

The monkeys grabbed for the fruit but _____ couldn't reach it.

14 Circle two words in the group in which ch makes the same sound:

school   cheap

chemistry   chalet

15 Underline the correctly spelt word:

sovereighn   sovereign   sovereyn

16 Choose the correct verb to complete the sentence:

Our water bottles was / were / is empty long before we reached the river.

17 Add the suffix ation to turn this verb into a noun:

punctuate   _____

18 Circle the word you would find first in a dictionary:

adjective   adjust   adjacent

19 Add a third word to this word family:

attract   attraction   _____

20 Circle four errors in this sentence:

'It's to early for the bats to be out, said the explorer' inpatiently.

How did you do?   1–5 Try again   6–10 Good try!
11–15 Great work!   16–20 Excellent exploring!

/20

Explorer's Logbook

Tick off the topics as you complete them and then colour in the star.

How do you feel?
- Needs practice
- Nearly there
- Got it!

Super suffixes ☐

Untangling tenses ☐

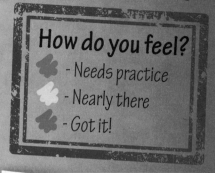

Totally <u>a</u>dverbs ☐

Tricky letter strings ☐

Changing words ☐

Daring dictionaries ☐

Exploring ou sounds ☐

Wild word endings ☐

Perfect proofreading ☐

Applying apostrophes ☐

Adding information ☐

Time to talk! ☐

i or *y* spelling? ☐

Sentences, sorted! ☐

Exploring *ch* words ☐

Devilish homophones! ☐

Choosing verbs ☐

Wild word families ☐

Making nouns ☐

Perfect pronouns ☐

Answers

Pages 2–3
Task 1
a digital   **b** referral   **c** preferring
d labelled   **e** shovelled   **e** clarify
Task 2
a conference   **b** levelled   **c** beginning
d differing   **e** regretting
Task 3
a chiselled   **b** referral   **c** forgotten
d marvellous   **e** solidify   **f** transferred
Exploring Further

L	A	S	A	H	A	B	I	T	U	A	L	S
A	O	R	B	I	M	R	R	A	R	R	I	R
C	N	D	T	S	E	O	I	R	W	O	O	D
C	P	E	O	T	P	E	D	G	T	W	P	E
I	M	N	T	I	D	D	E	E	E	J	R	N
M	N	A	C	R	D	E	A	T	S	K	E	N
O	H	C	O	I	E	L	D	E	G	U	F	E
C	A	T	N	C	R	O	L	D	H	E	E	T
L	A	R	K	C	I	R	U	W	E	Y	R	R
E	P	O	C	A	C	T	Y	O	E	R	R	O
W	Y	H	I	L	Q	A	T	U	G	M	H	H
G	F	S	H	R	R	P	I	N	G	E	D	S

HABITUAL ✓ – HISTIRICCAL ✗
TARGETED ✓ – TROPICCAL ✗
SHREDDED ✓ – SHORTENNED ✗
PINGED ✓ – PATROLED ✗
CHATTER ✓ – COMICCAL ✗

Pages 4–5
Task 1
a crypt   **b** hysterical
c flint   **d** cyst
Task 2
a gym   **b** rhythm   **c** wriggle
d syrup   **e** kilt   **f** hyphen
g flinch   **h** oxygen   **i** links
Task 3
a Platypuses   **b** physical   **c** mysterious
d mythology   **e** symbol
Exploring Further
gypsy, lyric, onyx, typical, syllable

Pages 6–7
Task 1
a tour   pour
b mouth   mouse
c couple   double
d you   crouton
e various   famous
Task 2
a Groops (Groups)   **b** curios (curious)   **c** mouch (much)
d tuch (touch)   **e** befour (before)
Task 3
a town   **b** saver   **c** allowed
d hoop   **e** tower   **f** truth
g floor   **h** older
Exploring Further
a HOUR   **b** SHOUT   **c** HOUSE
d YOUNG   **e** FLAVOUR

Pages 8–9
Task 1
a disagree   **b** irresponsible   **c** indecisive
d irreplaceable   **e** illegible
Task 2
a impolite   **b** misbehave   **c** inedible
d illegal   **e** irregular   **f** undeniable

Task 3
a unfortunate   **b** improbable   **c** disentangle
Exploring Further
Across   Down
1. illogical   2. inactive
3. misinformed   4. unfair
5. irresponsible   6. impolite

Pages 10–11
Task 1
a been   **b** hear   **c** see
d by   **e** be
Task 2
a write   **b** source   **c** our
d some   **e** You're
Task 3
a soar, sore   **b** pore, paw or poor
c vain, vein   **d** reign, rein
e road, rowed   **f** cord, cored or cawed
Exploring Further
a pare - to cut off the outer layer of something
b pair – two of something
c steel - a type of metal
d steal - to take without permission
e wail - a loud cry
f whale – a large sea mammal

Pages 12–13
Task 1
a session   **d** tension
b musician   **e** admission
c ration   **f** incision
Task 2
a expansion   **d** action
b politician   **e** intention
c discussion   **f** completion
Task 3
Any sentence is acceptable which uses each word in its
correct context.
Exploring Further
passion, intention, protection, adaptation, reaction

Pages 14–15
Task 1
a kiwi's   **b** explorers'   **c** zoologist's
d Kiwis'   **e** sun's
Task 2
explorers', ships, it's, sailors', storms'
Task 3

Singular	Plural
a woman's bag	two women's bags
a rabbit's ears	two rabbits' ears
a person's health	two people's health
a country's flag	two countries' flags
a child's toy	two children's toys
a man's key	two men's keys
a monkey's tail	two monkeys' tails

Exploring Further
Correct sentences are **a** and **d**

Pages 16–17
Task 1
a timidly   **b** brightly
c silently   **d** safely
Task 2
a happily   **b** simply
c prettily   **d** merrily
e hungrily   **f** irritably
g greedily   **h** busily

Task 3
Answers will vary. Accept any that include a suitable adverb.
Exploring Further
Any sentence is acceptable which uses the words in an appropriate context.

Pages 18–19
Task 1
a after **b** because
c so **d** when
Task 2
a because **b** if
c until **d** while
Task 3
Possible answers include:
a before **b** when
c if **d** although
Exploring Further
Any sentence ending is acceptable which follows on sensibly from the sentence opening.

Pages 20–21
Task 1
a high in a tree
b At nightfall
c until she was exhausted
d As she watched
e High in the sky
Task 2
a After the storm, we set off back to camp.
b In the trees, the birds shook the rain from their feathers.
c An hour later, the sun came out.
d All around us, steam rose from the glossy leaves of plants.
e Above us, the birds began to sing.
Task 3
a In Australia, bush fires are quite common.
b In bush fires, slow animals like koalas can be injured.
c After the fire, many koalas were taken to wildlife hospitals.
Exploring Further
a Despite their name, koala bears are not really bears.
b As land is cleared for farming, koalas' habitats are being lost.
c Preferring certain types of eucalyptus leaves, koala bears are fussy eaters.

Pages 22–23
Task 1
a The zoologist exclaimed, 'This water is so muddy, I can't see a thing!'
b Her guide replied, 'The frogs will be hiding in the mud.'
c 'Have you ever seen one?' asked the zoologist.
d 'I'm afraid not,' admitted her guide.
Task 2
Direct speech: **a**, **b**, **d**.
Reported speech: **c**, **e**.
Task 3
Possible answers include:
a exclaimed **b** asked
c replied **d** admitted
Exploring Further
Any answer is acceptable which uses appropriate direct speech for the context of the sentence, with inverted commas in the correct places.

Pages 24–25
Task 1
a have loved
b have enlarged
c have enchanted
d has visited
Task 2
Present perfect tense: **b**, **c**, **e**.
Task 3
a has studied
b has spent
c has seen
d has written

Exploring Further

	Present perfect form	Simple past
a	has discovered	discovered
b	has known	knew
c	has gone	went
d	has been	was
e	has flown	flew

Pages 26–27
Task 1
a they **b** it **c** she
d I **e** me
Task 2
a they **b** us **c** it
d we **e** you
Task 3
a He decided to explore because he loved wildlife.
b They lifted stones gently to see if they could find mini-beasts.
c We are often afraid of spiders, but perhaps they are afraid of us too!
Exploring Further
Any sensible interpretation of the sentence is acceptable.
Possible answers include:
The children bought their teachers presents but left the gifts in the classroom.

Pages 28–29
Task 1

chief	choir	chandelier
channel	chemist	chef

Task 2
a brochure **b** scheme **c** cashier
d shambles **e** parachute **f** chaotic
Task 3
a monarch **b** moustache **c** cricket
e character **e** camouflage **f** chauffeur
Exploring Further

M	A	C	H	I	N	E	A	C
A	C	H	E	H	U	T	E	H
C	M	A	S	H	E	T	R	A
H	E	S	T	O	M	A	C	H
U	L	E	C	K	O	C	H	G
T	C	H	S	E	C	H	O	E
E	S	T	E	L	K	O	P	H
S	T	O	M	A	C	K	C	K

Pages 30–31
Task 1
a weigh **b** prey
c they **d** neighbours
Task 2
a beige **b** feign **c** abseil
d osprey **e** convey
Task 3
Any sentence is acceptable that includes the given word in an appropriate context.
Exploring Further
a GREY **b** NEIGH **c** EIGHTY
d VEIL **e** SURVEY

Pages 32–33
Task 1
Correct sentences are: **c**, **e**, **f**.
Task 2
a I **b** are
c have **d** eat
Task 3
a are **b** sleep **c** need
d are **e** have
Exploring Further
a she was   they were
b I live   he lives
c she will   we will

d he loves   I love
e I am   you are
f they cry   he cries

Pages 34–35
Task 1
a temptation   **b** relaxation   **c** adoration
d variation   **e** admiration

Task 2
a imagination   **b** realisation   **c** revelation
d sensation   **e** inspiration

Task 3
a despair   **b** apply   **c** occupy
d oblige   **e** register

Exploring Further
1 continuation   **2** condensation   **3** formation
4 preparation   **5** combination

Pages 36–37
Task 1
a forest   **b** mountain   **c** animal
d difficulty   **e** transport

Task 2
a burrow, nest, sett
b firefly, hedgehog, kiwi
c scorpion, tarantula, Tasmanian devil
d mole, moon, mountain

Task 3
Any word is acceptable which could be found between the pairs of words given.

Exploring Further
crab, crack, creak, crease, create, creature

Pages 38–39
Task 1
a service, servant   **b** recycle, cyclical
c numerate, numeral   **d** extended, extensive
e circular, circumference

Task 2
a treaty   **b** chilled   **c** flue
d award   **e** access

Task 3
Possible answers include:
a dancer   **b** healthy   **c** received
d growth   **e** angry

Exploring Further

S	H	A	O	T	O	A	M	R	K
T	H	E	E	S	F	A	R	E	T
M	I	L	B	E	A	L	A	S	H
O	D	S	U	L	M	N	L	E	I
A	D	D	I	T	I	O	N	A	M
N	E	P	L	V	L	I	O	R	I
A	N	L	T	L	I	C	A	C	E
T	S	K	E	O	A	B	L	H	T
L	E	O	D	P	R	E	A	T	H

Pages 40–41
Task 1
a I found some <u>informacian</u> about where to locate Humboldt squid. information.
b We sailed <u>sowth</u> across the ocean. south.
c As we <u>traveled</u>, I made notes of the creatures we saw. travelled.
d The cries of seagulls <u>eccoed</u> through the air. echoed.
e At night we saw squid <u>greedyly</u> gobbling up tiny fish. greedily.

Task 2
a Last night, we searched for a shoal of squid.
b 'This is wonderful!' exclaimed the explorer.
c The zoologist suggested, ' Let's explore the ocean.'
d Three explorers' hats blew away in the storm.

Task 3
a guest – guessed   **b** scene – seen   **c** your – you're
d inn – in   **e** its – it's

Exploring Further
Answers as follows:
It was <u>regretable</u> <u>too</u> <u>here</u> of your <u>intension</u> to abandon <u>you're</u> search <u>four</u> the Humboldt squid. I hope your decision will not be <u>finle</u> and that you will change your <u>mined</u>. <u>Its</u> not <u>to</u> late!
There are 10 mistakes.

Answers to quick test
1 metallic
2 crystal
3 roudy
4 incapable
5 scent
6 station, electrician, mission
7 The <u>mens</u>' torches cast shadows on the cave's walls.
8 prettily
9 because
10 In the morning, we set off again on our journey.
11 'I'll record my discovery in my notebook,' said the explorer.
12 has trekked
13 they
14 school, chemistry
15 sovereign
16 were
17 punctuation
18 adjacent
19 Possible answers include: attractive
20 Change to to too; move the inverted comma to between out, and said; insert a comma after explorer; change inpatiently to impatiently